WHITE COINS

OTHER PUBLICATIONS BY THE AUTHOR:

Passages of Time (Flipped Eye, 2002)
Voice Recognition: 21 Poets for the 21st Century
(co-editor, Bloodaxe, 2009)
Blood / Sugar (Arc Publications, 2009)
The Wolf: A Decade 2002-2012
(editor, Wolf Editions, 2012)
Bones Will Crow: 15 Contemporary Burmese Poets
(co-editor, Arc Publications, 2012)
Soapboxes (Knives, Forks and Spoons, 2014)
Myth of the Savage Tribes, Myth of Civilised Nations
(in collaboration with Sandeep Parmar,
Oystercatcher, 2014)
Everything that is Broken Up Dances
(forthcoming with Tupelo Press, USA)

White Coins
JAMES BYRNE

2015

Published by Arc Publications
Nanholme Mill, Shaw Wood Road,
Todmorden OL14 6DA, UK
www.arcpublications.co.uk

Copyright © James Byrne, 2015
Copyright in the present edition © Arc Publications, 2015
Design by Tony Ward
Printed by TJ International, Padstow, Cornwall

978 1908376 47 3 (pbk)
978 1908376 48 0 (hbk)
978 1908376 49 7 (ebook)

ACKNOWLEDGMENTS

The author is grateful to the editors of the following magazines and websites in which some of these poems, or versions of these poems, first appeared: *3am, Agenda, archiveofthenow.org, Axon, Black Herald, Eyewear, International Times, The International Literary Quarterly, Litmus, Paris Lit. Up Magazine, Poetry Wales, Stand, The Nation* and *The North*.

'Primitive Culture' consists of excerpts from a collaborative poem with Sandeep Parmar entitled 'Myth of the Savage Tribes, Myth of Civilised Nations' published in *Island Magazine* (Australia) and also in a jointly authored pamphlet with the same title (Oystercatcher Press, 2014). 'Soapbox' was originally published as 'Soapbox 4' in *Soapboxes*, a pamphlet by Knives, Forks and Spoons Press (2014). A version of 'On the Ordinary' was first published in *The Wolf* (30), as an editorial piece.

The author also wishes to thank the Arts Council England for giving him a grant to complete this book and John Wedgwood Clarke for his editorial suggestions on the manuscript.

Cover image:
'The Last Sound' by Ibrahim El-Salahi,
by kind permission of the artist.
From the private collection of Abdul Magid Breish.
© Ibrahim El-Salahi. All rights reserved, DACS 2015

This book is in copyright. Subject to statutory exception and to provision of relevant collective licensing agreements, no reproduction of any part of this book may take place without the written permission of Arc Publications.

**Editor for the UK and Ireland
John W. Clarke**

for Sandeep Parmar

CONTENTS

I

Historia / 11
Economies of the Living
    Tender Mothers / 17
    Brothers and Sisters / 18
    Simulation / 19
    Benevolence / 20
    The Eagle / 21
    The Hummingbird / 22
    The Horse / 23
    The Orangutan / 24
    Mortality / 25
    Immortality / 26
    Heaven / 27
River Nocturnes / 28
Philomela in Paris / 32
Divorce ~~Pending~~ / 36
Primitive Culture / 37
The Boy / 41
Breakfast / 42
The Nook (exterior) / 43
~~Self~~ Portrait / 44
Drink / 45
Summons / 46
Home / 47

II

Diagnosis Inc. / 51
Phrase & Fable
    To put a churl upon the house of a gentleman / 52
    Like sweet bells jangled out of tune and harsh / 53
    I'll soon settle his hash for him / 54
    To measure another's foot by your own last / 55

The thin red line / 56
Happy is the country that has no history / 57
The Pure Nation / 58
Pauperland / 59
Soapbox / 60
On the Ordinary / 62
Consultancy / 66
from Middlesex Hospital / 68
The Footage / 70
Foodstuffs / 71
All Mouth / 73
Rimbaud Villanelles
   14 Rue Nicolet / 74
   Scarborough / 75
   8 Royal College Street / 76
Inside the House of Lu San / 77
Your Toad / 78
Playlist
   Monsieur Le Maire De Niafunké / 79
   Mariama / 81
   Kala Djula / 82
   Yombe / 83
   Cheikh Anta / 84

Notes / 85
Biographical Note / 87

I

HISTORIA

> moving on or going back to where you came from
> AMY CLAMPITT

> it is not the substance of a man's fault
> it is the shape of it
> is what lives with him, is what shows
> CHARLES OLSON

a room crammed   with sharp toys

a field zesty with fire

    history as historia

  cool as a shot to the mouth

      *

            in pinched shoes
              cataleptic

         merely to show up

     the birdlime viscidity of the garden
     the scalpel-like finger
        of a shrivelled leaf—

    not accusatory
              shadowed only
                  by itself
    not pointing
  towards a balance-act
          but balancing

*

I was six and made of violins
                          stumped
                by metronomic light

  I wanted to energise him away
     like glucose
         globed
     into whiteness—

    a voice spoken slantwise
          but faraway—

              sleeping it off

        I travelled in the dark
        so as not to be seen

*

  dusk-nervousness
    in what is   unclaimed

I wait and fail
    paying off warders
        at your door—

              the thrillbox
              of birthdays

     whalecalls from waterclotted
        condensation

            the gazebladed kitchen

        the uplander silences of television

                    blackish fingernails
                            from window-mould

            eyes goggled
                    towards a lit hearth
                        fringe fraying

            or cupping at the curtain frame
                    fearful of fire
                        on the domestic zodiac

        *

        how the air divides
                like cutting a loaf—

    as much childed
            as fevered

                    left alone
                in the dry season

    to feed from the day's nutrients—

                            naphtha mirage
                                over the wheatfield
                                    at sunset

                    foxfur grinning on a spidersweb

                    dialysis of rain
                              inside a garden well

                    equal to breath

              *

     —to hear the substance of the earth
                    to know its shape

              blessèd as an egg
     and yet—

              and yet bombarded
                    by the radio impulse
                         of survival

              the whistlework of money—

her ivied hair
     trenched at the oven or
     admonished at the fire-grate

              *

shuffle-worn cards
                    blanked-out letters
                         from the on-dead

how life tickles the palm
     at twenty

      dreaming up worser devils

thinking the lesser disease might be
                            loneliness—

no-one to ignite
        the red-eyed bird
           of your mind

no-one told you why
                love
                    blunts

    *

if the bones sing

if chaos is chaos
      returned—

                        no atom nuclei
      no definitive cure

    *

enter fortune

      a ransacked house
            half-emptied—

that which remains
preserved in boxes

                    now bulges
                like a museum

                        *

baffled voices   vow trounces
   —as if from any archive—

I lean over and touch my ear
    to the grid complex—

                like hearing ritual cannibalism
                    in the byways of a river

ECONOMIES OF THE LIVING

Tender Mothers

Mark the parent who is violent
by choice. Who—like the kite—
hovers, hypnotised by its prey.

To be borne off by black talons,
she stands in front of you again,
someone to administer the sickness.

She, the wingspan of your accent.
The maunderer of your gratitude.
Patient hen, thundered by quarrels.

BROTHERS AND SISTERS

But you are not filial of one father.
Go to the desert and observe the stork
of wilderness. Its rustles and sobs.

Blood bangs against the economy
of life. Brothers and sisters should be
sweeter than Persian incense offered

to the sun. You were born with the dusk
in your hair, deaf to slander, covertly
watching film behind closed eyelids.

SIMULATION

Dear docile one, love instruction.
Love the tenor of retreat and Seneca
who exhorted youth for probity.

In this age of bitter imprudence,
severity displeases Instagram.
Faulty preceptors, esteem synthesis.

Where the labourer is like fashion—
sown, but not reaping the seed. Where
the tv plays alone in blue-lit rooms.

BENEVOLENCE

Considerest thy buried wants. Consider
Freud's iceberg versus knowing thyself.
Endued, despite the desire for good.

Old habits clustering as if for humour.
You who once rioted against every
means of convenience, hold communion

now with yourself, fowl of air, novice
philosopher. You who flattered himself
to think that thinking qualifies action.

THE EAGLE

Yeats in his psychopomp. Blavatsky
a lion among quadrapets. Similitudes.
As if accolades were lofty as cliffs.

Maud Gonne pursued, but as worthy
conquest? I would rather be a falcon
or rook, with mischief to provoke her.

Brother, remember how we cast ourselves
as children carried off by Scottish eagles.
Found affrighted but reclaimed by parents.

The Hummingbird

Hazelnut. Feathered black, brownish and green. Traitor to the flower press, luxuriant but uselessly sportive, uselessly fluttering.

Female's the architect. Male: a panicked fetcher of cottoned twigs, vegetable fibres. Skivvy for cloudhouses suspended in air.

A family of silken music caged by Labat for rats. We are purposed for pleasure. Touch the wings to kill its instrument.

The Horse

Europe's incommode: it is not free
to roam continents like the horse did.
Tack, yield, never knowing winter.

Turnstiled like prisoners of the sedan.
Tractable and familiar. The Bedouin
shares his tent with foals, surrenders

his courser mare to the French consul.
The things a horse has traded for gold.
Closely farried, shockpools for eyes.

The Orangutan

Brute like us. Brute of the woods.
Sternly countenanced then maligned
like cracked hutches of the counselled.

Epitaphic, ritualized buriers and so
larger than most men. Upwards of you
unfolding a napkin and as Buffon said:

fond of comfits but, unlike the baboon,
clever to show a man where the door is.
Trained servants, able to work as we do.

MORTALITY

What makes for strong pillars? Roots
like crooked fangs and the spectacle
of letting blood. Those Nietzchean debts

collected, as if to pay what you owe
were pure as the horizoned backdrop
to some Parthenonic theatre. Death

is in the world, stand up, weep together
or longer. Insects sport all day in the sun.
Easterly winds nip the verdure nightlong.

IMMORTALITY

Yesterday's shadow cocked like a trigger.
Buds newly-crown the brooding branches.
Trumpets echo before and after him.

None of these things bid the dead awake.
I will watch the raked light of sunset
over Shardeloes and find you via memory.

Speak. Tell me the story of his hands
bound by Blake-light, a thousand angels.
I would marry her forever and again.

Heaven

Life is good and there's plenty of it.
Hymnals of rose and thorn. Henbane
doesn't bloodspeckle the white lilacs.

Barbauld saw heaven with cherubim
flying on fired wings. Borges craved
endless library shelves. Hold on hope.

Son of Jesse, shepherd king, with what
language do we say goodbye to ourselves?
What bell sings another hour of her?

RIVER NOCTURNES

    1.

(Scrub moon requitals)

        Gemming white flints pearl up
        a transmutable necklace—

            presage of jade
                as if Ferris-powered

      watercrowned / watercorridored
at the dock berth

        the river snaked by
            a wash of marble

Plashed stone for the veinwork
      to disembody—

           jellyroll vortex of grey buildings

                a face crashing
                      immemorially
                into the shook river

2.

Antiquated maelstrom in silhouette

    (the self slaloming
        ceremonially with the tide
            —such psychical deceptions!)

Shadows refract under streetlamps

    a bankside of mock Narcissi
                spurs
    the body as mothshadow—
          its blackmirror outline
        clinically disperses at the quay

Here light is fluxive
(yet trainable as any acrobat)

        scientifically (*and* non-scientifically) agile

once curiously positioned

        it is barely tangible

3.

Overly astringent
    so as to hoodwink
        into weatherlessness—

            the sulphury harbour air
            the smokish rain
                reflect
            zenith distances—

water-fringed swale-markers
    in a skyscape that is translatable
only as the mood turns

        (vision to mind   a *language*
        on repeat)

But how to paint it in   (the *movement*)

        labyrinth trails in a sonical stormlash
    pronged overexposure of lightning
        a skybull stamping out spherical thunder

The after-echo crackles off to sea

        traded in the City
            for pincered rain—
        a pincushion under Greenwich causeway

How to paint it in
        to annihilate the merest anchor point

4.

(Is she the supreme humanist
    moving among inhuman faces
or a shivery pythoness)

      Her gildedness concealed
          by the Barrier's silver-rodded orbs
        where an ashy cloud door
           lingers
  like a brooding jury

        until
        verdictless

            doubles open

PHILOMELA IN PARIS

    1.

From Thracian voyages
        to the immortal bird of Keats
                to a mustardy café in Monceau

a Pisse Vieille aggrieves the palate
      like a tapestry
             impossible to scrub clean—

the admixture appropriates   latitudinally
      restaging a scene from the Parc's follies

where Philomela's song engages
        the hawk-tailed Luftwaffe pilot—
            his enrolled horror
                  his chevron boasts

2.

How later she knew   unconsolatory joy
not for Paris   returning to its pleasure canvas

            —free boats wreathing the Seine
                    workers steadying up
                            refastening jackboots—

Not for any man
        more the quick and the raw—
lost armies of women   shaven-headed
                             mutilated
                             stripped

            recovered from the grave
                    to their own cities

3.

From the Café des Deux Moulins
    she lay on a bed   defiled
            speechless

occupied by the feast
    of an orphanable child—

hernia grief's re-echoing   the crackwhip—
    the bird-brained
        absence maker of man—

    who thinks himself higher than a god
    living in the exact centre of the world

Through the curtain cuff a storm hoods Rue Murillo

    thundercrash like a rock from Hades—
    birth cries loosen the oil of a doorframe

4.

Born to rumour   to the hostilities of invention—
      inaudible chatter behind a wall-length door
            at St. Suplice

            a Tereusian double in the Quai de Grenelle
                  swept and afflicted by
                        the rebound of its own shadow—

1943   Father   German
the child newspapered   'horizontal collaboration'

Along the Parc promenade
      brisking through a swallow's two notes
            his stout cry channels hemlock
      from her cut chords

            ferments Procne—

                  I have weaved you a robe of blood
            she would say
                  sister my sister

DIVORCE ~~PENDING~~

Pending the thinning out of this highwire
and proposals over the matrimonial home
or if there's a shove at the new servant and
if the squirrel trove might go unaccounted
along with all the usual indemnities without
prejudice and provisions based on further
joint conduct and pending the death of man
or wife in sickness and in health to death
do them part etcetera etcetera but no matter
who played curdy-curd or who lived through
a midlife of kitchens and who pushed who
from a moving car to shield the moneypot
—revert to section 27 pending further orders
all null should the client earn x per annum—
to be accepted forthwith in lieu of outgoings
or company loans and pending gross assets
net profit in relation to property / mortgages
/ court fees and the public claims of pensions
or the antenuptial arm-twist and the scarscab
settling over two lives that girded like blood

PRIMITIVE CULTURE

Spring Break '85
Dancing on Ice
Wembley Arena
Auntie Sandra's encoded theatre
of compliance
and the animal of my grandfather
locked in a razored glare
fixed on the sequinned show
of the figureskate
only to pool us in

>*look at the coon
>a darkie John Travolta*

And with this my grandfather
Henry—flinchless before the ice
and in the deadly seat of his pillory—
twiddles his handlebar tash
opens the flint-furnace of his mouth
and splits inside his own laughter

>[blood vertigos the brain
>fistballs in an open palm]

From *racoon*?
from the Portuguese
barracoos
—sale house for bartered slaves—
or George Dixon
aka Dixie Coon
blackface minstrel dandy stagenamed

Zip Coon
singing 'Coal Black Rose'

> *Lubly Rosa Sambo cum*
> *dont you hearde Banjo*
> *tum tum tum...*
> *Oh Rose der coal black Rose*

Meet the hand of your friend at the hawthorn
grandfather
his song scalds the devil's water
and you are with him—
unsunk stone
of time and hate

At Loftus Road
in the family stand
his gorilla-grunting noises
my bodywell of panic—
moistened underarms
as my grandfather scuffles
with a Jamaican pensioner
from Liverpool—
the crowd swivels its thousand heads
to face us

> [buried mirror of my face
> dilated hieroglyphs of eye]

I would introduce you to my grandmother
but now at her last
in the iron of cancer?

Dark bile in her voice
on meeting strangers
throne of scrutinizing glances—

she would look you over
not as a granddaughter
but some kind of voodoo

> '...the fetish woman answers in a thin, whistling voice,
> and with the old-fashioned idioms of generations past.'
>
> (E.B. Tylor, *Primitive Culture*, Vol. 2)
>
> The Duke of Wellington—describing his own army—
> 'The scum of the Earth. The mere scum of the Earth'.

When the first Pakistani family
moved into Narcott Lane
she turned over the face
of a new brown baby
and shook like a burning tree
and said to her Henry

> *s'like aliens off a spaceship*
> *landed in our own backyard—*

the child woke from sea-sleep
his mother petrified into flame

'There is a forgotten,
nay almost forbidden word,
which means more to me than any other.
That word is England'

(Winston Churchill)

Phil came back from the Navy
with a wincy Sri-Lankan thing
didn't speak a word
black as a spade
she sat on the front lawn
all morning
all day
cross-legged
half-naked
kindness past one like that…
…tapped 'n the head I said
poor Phil
I said
I said to 'im
you be kind to yourself
you'll be kind to 'er

'…where barbaric hordes groped blindly,
cultured men can often move onward with clear view.
It is a harsher, and at times even painful, office of ethnography
to expose the remains of crude old culture
which have passed into harmful superstition,
and to mark these out for destruction.'

(*Primitive Culture*, Vol. 2)

THE BOY

See the boy under a brick-shadowed banister
scratching at the identity card of his own face.

See the boy in a tangle of roots, ever-uprooted,
dreaming he was born to a three-headed ibis.

A sudden rain wakes the wind, crashes the eaves
and palliates the voices of a couple wrangling

over their lives. See him docked now at the island
of childhood, astonished by the saltiness of blood,

or bartering with the seller of scars, to be outbid,
tarried by the stillpoint of the unfinished moment.

BREAKFAST
: *for Sandeep*

A cloud of geese telegraphs the sky,
ten-laned and trembling our birdbath.
The broken pane reflects crowfooted
sinews, an earned face, a jag of wires.

Sun's tinder, the width of matchsticks,
severs our curtain, lights the coffeepot
smoking like a gun. My savage hands
disturbing the pique of your dream.

THE NOOK (EXTERIOR)

Hay sails the road's moat.
Over a dark mile of corn,

a far field burns,
wakes the sleeping village.

Propeller density of sirens.
Flames hiss my ears.

Cloud's ardour, how could I
better distil you? Shadowed by pines,

I squat behind an apple tree,
smoking grandmother's menthols.

Late apples moulder like dough.
The rot smells of vermouth.

Each branch stencils the sun.
Straw and ash fly the wind.

SELF PORTRAIT

The conundrums in a face,
the infeuds. Eggways-profiled,
atomized for complexity—
self-czarism, self-censurism.

But marked and marked again,
altar-points, mintings of light
and shadow. The inquisitorial eye
churns away like a granary.

I call back a day of sparse blues,
eavesdropping on a lit field.
There is room for a cut breeze.
The clouds show no signs of ageing.

DRINK

Let's have a drink and clear the halo of the glass
and clear the haloes of watercubes from the glass.

I meet your eye and cheers and check for poisons—
enemy, family, stool friend, Celtish at the table,

if genealogy's all canker, mine's a double-double.
Let's drink to bloodscoot, the bonnys, the dumps,

with gold eyes lighting up in dark rooms, in secret,
among scareheads who detonate the private cloud.

Who knew, so much in common. You are my animal,
my grotto song. Your fire's tremolo frills my shivers.

SUMMONS

On the grapevine shadow of a table,
a spook, a summons.

Unlike us, equable as money
and patient to sentiment. Sent, as if

from the wind's only daughter
or England's infant rivers,

plum over the forbidding seal—
a word loaded like a killer's bullet.

HOME

They said I came out with a thorn in my foot—
hillcloud child who spoke with a large name,
blossy among broken hedges and molten fields.

When the house hellbelled I retouched an image
of hyaline mists gridlocked to corn. The memory
of sky over Pankridge Farm held like a salve.

I listened to the beginning patience in a voice
until it was clamant, exasperated to pure nerve—
'Home' it repeated. 'Home. Come home'.

II

DIAGNOSIS INC.

You are two oranges shy of sangria
You chumpchange in a clackdish
You the flensed soldier, egg-runny on the inside
You frogging deadline after deadline
You caught in a Swiss chokehold
You feeding the duckboards of Venice
You the expert on television newswar
You at maximum voice
You the squall above dead deerling
You the clarion-call of the id
You the barbaros of Juárez
You who want to wake up forever
You on page 65 in bubblegum PVC
You yelling at the meathook
You yet to make your wheelspin mark
You clapping at family stones
You who would rather be scalped standing
You as screw of the week
You eiderhanded as a spider
You in the stocks and wanting it more
You salted for planet jellyfish
You among the angels crisp as butcherpaper
You scissorless, cutting the line to ribbons
You the livid escarp
You the apostle of gutlove
You with a black and fraying candlestick
You hard to prove but terminally alluring
You an owl away from the topmost branch
You mad as a star
You who would shoot first

PHRASE & FABLE

To put a churl upon the house of a gentleman

Yards of yarn to measure churlish gentlemen
doesn't recast them beyond fables of drinking
beer after wine or Grenville's 'Gentle Shepherd'—
his parliament buffoonery spoiling for blows
and spinning its own wool, circa 1763. Imagine
offering yourself up as satire to a brother-in-law
or being drunk daylong on excised cider. Grenville
bleated to the ministerial flock for years about
the freedomlessness of the press whilst doubling
national debt and sliding into his deathbed sheets.
How to override history? To 'churl' reverbs me
back to an abandoned mural on Cookson Street—
a scythian wind rapped at houses, but there was
no window trivia, only jokes without punchlines.

Like sweet bells jangled out of tune and harsh

Who's there? Sound of whips and scorns for you,
brother at the empty door. Panicked, pigeon-livered,
you were a boy once, a tiddler with a latchkey, until
your father moved inside the photo like a chessman.
Who's there, who's there? Enter Ghost of three bells,
breadcrumbs for intemperance. At night insomnal
as a dogwatch, the street steals you piece by piece.
Shadowy mischief inside the core of an apple tree,
nature as informant, gadflies of radio surveillance.
The CD pause / rewind / plays on a loop, exuding
alter egos: Ted and Zippy—childhood animations
storyboarded, but out of sync. As if the heart's tabla
struck jail metal or daily vita muffled a passing bell.
Loud bark of hell's labrador—*harsh* is a euphemism.

I'll soon settle his hash for him

After rehashing him, making mincemeat of him,
running his schemes and goose-cooking him, about
the same time the earls went as mad as their castles,
but not the exactsame time I heard the byword for
donkey in Arabic—jahash or jahsh?—also means
idiot. Lost inside memory's boombox, on the steps
of Paris' Club de Hashisheen, hashballs fermenting us
like a street cry (I remember hashing up Bauderlaire
to the factSPACE of Olson and moving my mouth
like it were counterwound between marvel and sense).
Or that time you asked if everything is Iraq re-hashed
like the rest of the world might say to America: 'come
catch me or kill my neighbour'. Hash defined as cut
meat or—like war is—something old served up new.

To measure another's foot by your own last

Like politicians first-footing on humanitarian issues,
foreign policy is a butcher, reflective as its blade.
Hide history's measuring tape, the battlefield chemists
and dioxin hotspots, the attics of clumsy gas masks—
too many able laboratory fires and scorched calendars.
The figures skew on those carried out feet foremost.
To calculate you'd be a clayfoot, there's good reason
no-one's tried to measure a country by the size of its feet.
Foreign policy dictates to always find one's own feet
before putting the boot down upon the neck. As if
chemical rhetoric were like limbering up for a Roman
footrace. Reprints of Chemical Ali, Kerry fox-feinting
with Lavrov, cloven-hoofed mediations from Russia—
all formulas must be stockpiled before incineration.

The thin red line

It has been drawn, redrawn, crosshatched and cross-stitched. Before the Battle of Balaclava before wind engraved the sand, lines were marking out countries, splitting fig leaves, dividing partition houses (the rule: that what lies between lines must be toed to the line or else rears the face of death's cherub). They draw a line because a circle is too comely. Perhaps this is why Russell's highlanders marshalled a thin red line instead of a square, or why blood grooved the axis-points on cheekbones of Yumans at the Yuma River, lacquered on with spit and piss. Shoot me a line, show me a fair line-up. Cryptographies, nightdarks. You don't know about the alternating lines of my life. Look at the way the colonials divided tribes into lots.

Happy is the Country That Has No History

A register of mankind marked by enisled historians.
Human error propagates, every horror assails and
pokerfaces upstage catacombs. It's all about gaming
stakes for power, emissaries as guarantors—enquiry
after enquiry sweeps the showrooms of the kapital.
You said you wanted happiness, but events divert us.
Sniff over scentless flowers, under Apollyonic stars.
We can turn ourselves into giant birds via aviatrix.
And I too sought happiness but how many whites is
white and when did whiteness become something filthy?
They still ridicule Lennon's 'Imagine' (even Paul saw
John as painting his own cradle) and the pantisocratic
dream of Coleridge shattered him. History revolves
on powerplays: who to tread the wine, who to drink it?

THE PURE NATION
after Czeslaw Milosz

Whose forcefield is irretractable as a suburban king

Who is cityless and the nutritious dirt on a microscope

Exulted by Hegel at the moment he mortgaged his soul

The golden generation subsists on a menu of breadrinds

The auctioneers prefer impressionist florals

Art as a bidding war equal to the pure nation

Who would birdcage Beethoven as a mere romantic

Who say: 'another language means blood in the ears'

They sloganeer contingency plans as the great leap

They claim the brothel matron will design a brooch from it

Inside every house they are looking for somewhere to live

PAUPERLAND
after Jeremy Seabrook

Power being reverence   cut a hand   it bleeds
But DO NOT DISTURB   the fart stench of your soul

Immiserated   numb as an Electric Ray-
Self-subverted   for a share of the privies

Scopa before beesting   Logic of repetition
Like a mirror stockading fire   or the shadow

Inside a window of white moon   Picking thorns
In Cottonopolis   in offal backstreets

Featherbedding pleonexia   parish pay-tables
Temples under temples   where bodiless priests

Feign talkback with a charmed god   who does not
Speak to them through clouds but on a testoon's face

Sound of money meaning   sound governance
As if our skins stuck to each other   only the poor

Feared as feral to the hour   Austerity's bogeywoman
Haunting her own neighbourhoods   Pickled

As the something-must-be-done   or done towards
To bridge the dignities of avarice   Florin makers

And Ducats who would keep still a month of doubters
To kickback against a lifetime   plundered as stocks

SOAPBOX

the baron's son hotfoots
the dogshit-shoe-shuffle

pendulum to debtor
           creditor
spleenlessness
        unceasing in Cain fires
how the camouflage deepens—

      scintilla of thorns
           in the hedgerow
a face hidden behind
      constitutional pillars

the human by-product
      predictive as taxonomy

the prudential supervision—
      stockjobbers humming
          like a field of locusts

quicksilvering munition loot
      for petro chips
the anonymity of banknotes   cartelisations
      of the Royal Mint

to be unsatiated   to disappear
      on arms receipts   into
          parachute blankets
          inflational lifeboats
          tomahawk diplomacy
        squarepegging boltholes—

Egyptian chevrons / Saudi princeships / Kazakh autocracies /
Greek dawns / Russian hooliganism / Burmese chalkboard /
Singaporean spyglass / American liberties / Israeli intifadas /
Nigerian *Shell*suits / Japanese waterworks / Chinese whispers

    &c. &c.   + infinitum

the baron's mouth flops open
    like a chequebook

ministerial PR
    claims monetarism =
        coined liberty

        not taxbrackets   monopoly pockets or
                                          shillings of laughter

        everywhereness
        of the particular
        where *greed is*
        go[o]*d*

the dark rollers
    print out
scant circulation

ON THE ORDINARY

> [Poets should] aim to engage with ordinary people much more. But I think poetry has rather connived at its own irrelevance [...] I'd like to see some sort of inquisition in which poets were called to account for their poetry and they had to appear before a panel of ordinary people to explain why they chose to write about the particular subject they chose to write about.
>
> Jeremy Paxman

On this cobbled bookshelf lives a street of ordinary lunatics. They are much like any family. Vallejo's lottery vendor keeps shouting up 'The Big One'. Mayakovsky un-purses the fire-licked door of his lips. Paz leans in my left ear still laughing over his ashes. Khoury-Ghata summons the rain's spokesman—mute fog—who, forgetting his usefulness, bellows fire.

The house is empty, but full of strange scents—Vedic wool, lamb-dankness of St. Kevin's kitchen. Someone is frying oiled saffron in the adjoining room.

Given any ordinary day I would write about how the rain combs like a harp. But I am various and distractible as anyone.

Inbox link to CNN airing five minutes on how to resuscitate a squirrel. Should you find one when cleaning out your backyard pool, rub three fingers and a thumb over its ribcage.

Autoclick: *How does an airport catch alight*? The U.S. (is it US?) offers to fly in SWATs. Click: domestic dust spreading internationally. England is a lost world (Littlejohn).

In Nigeria, the presidential mission has banned the 'BRING BACK OUR GIRLS' campaign. Relatives of passengers on board flight MH370 set up a whistleblower fund so that anyone (including government officials) can snitch.

How do an entire people lose themselves? Thurston: 'hidden language / sent down as heard'.

The pool cleaner advises against kissing a dying squirrel directly on the mouth. Just breathe gently over its nostrils. When the *little furry fella* wakes he coughs up what looks like a glob of wasabi.

These are extraordinary times.

*

Paxman's music is bowel music.

'Never love anyone who treats you like you're ordinary'.

Ordinary: *ordinarie, ordeinair,* genitive of *ordinaries*—'regular, usual, orderly'—genitive of *ordinis* from *ordo* meaning ORDER.

Out of order: those who are lost can be recovered. Out of the ordinary: that we might dare the benchers in Latin. Recycling scrubby textbooks for art.

Milton: 'a licencer should happ'n to be judicious more than ordinary'.

The world is a map. Jurisdictional ordinance. Laws of the Ordinary. Laws of Order (the Clarendon Code considered all thought a crime, if not in vestry interests).

Cartwright, mimicking Jonson, in 'The Song of the Ordinary Clubbers':

Then our Musick is in Prime,
When our teeth keep triple time;
Hungry Notes are fit for knels:
May lankeness be

No Quest to me.

*

This is how they fix you. Purity of white rocks against a haunch of black clouds.

Art is not the 'fixed or regulated sequence; occurring in the course of regular custom or practice; normal; customary; usual'. We are mysterious to ourselves.

I am a conniver in Apuleius' fancy dress. I coo over Kaminsky's pigeon music, peck the vengeful ears of Amba's calcine kingdoms. In winter, I waited with Césaire's garrotless snow leopard by the docks, bivouacked by history.

What is ordinary music? Who are the ordinary people?

Monk: 'Mr Paxman will be delighted to hear that henceforth I shall write exclusively for *ordinary* people and look forward to sales of my books going through the roof as UKIP voters queue to buy my poetry.'

Circus agencies for photo-ops: Farage balancing a Bombardier on his head.

The new order is the new ordinary. The bourgeoisie roll a double zero with cluedo dice.

Trotsky: 'Poetry is a free art and not a service to class'.

All people are either ordinary or extraordinary maniacs.

CONSULTANCY

Our consultant has the yellowing eyes of a lanneret and is about to berserk himself. The Longbar barman is out of his signature coffee (Aromatic Life 4, Addis Ababa). And our consultant (let's call him Edwin) wields a dice for sixes and the numbers undulate and we consult the sinking clay of his face and wonder if we might dial up the chief consultant at this hour for him to call in a proxy. But the line rings and rings on and Edwin, despite his bucket-black stare, is still remembered by us as a man who conjures the passion of an gnat and so it is our best chance to wait for him to (surely?) revive himself in this smelting house of assassins—a room crammed with other consultants, perhaps a hundred or more (the veritable cream of consultancy), who will not consult with us at any price even if they knew (and they do) that we were born to feed an island full of money. NO CAVORTING WITH THE OTHER CONSULTANTS reads the sign above The Longbar. And the cruel goddesses of variously identical waitresses (chiffoned red-black) pass us by to confirm that happy hour has begun and we should unrack our wallets. Save yourself with a double pitcher of Sunlight promises the crinkly blue menu and I hear the sound of my own laughter in the watery scales of the echoing room. As if there were some great or godly upper consultant who worked inside the sinews of bones and trees? Lameer (a specialist zebra trader from Natal) taps the shoulder of our consultant, Edwin, and offers him compensatory bribes from the African savanna—a furless baby zebra, a black-and-white-striped zebra rug and a harpoon weekend on his private ranch. Such things are from the wavecrest of the world, encourages Lameer. But Edwin plunges into television whiteness, a shepherd of the dead. He moves his mouth for what seems millennia but emits no sound. Mosaic calligraphy of speech. Poor Edwin the shadowless baby. I lave my throat with pink ginfizz and consider the aboutscene as befitting a world that is composed of two kinds: carrions and hunters, the nail and the poisoned tree, the caw and the crow. How we live out our unburied lives. Consultancy? It is just a job to do asserts Lameer and his wife agrees, shaking her porcelain hand in the air like the unremitting figure of a Chinese cat.

from **MIDDLESEX HOSPITAL**

For Sale: the mud-splotchy snipe-shoot at Farthing Pie House where—from a city's northerly outpost—the hospital's healing acreage (its herbaceous gardens) 'rose in the midst of a swamp'.

Returned to the ratting pit, leagues of underground dissection rooms, soiled because of UCH economic deuces (the hospital never wanted to merge with the University). Mortimer Street's terracotta pomp razed, then loggerheaded to the premise of an abandoned excavation site.

For Sale: a 999-year lease brokered and signed during millipede rounds at the Bear and Rummer Publick House. The backbreaking cadgework (circa 1755) which appealed to patrons/landowners/aristocrats, for an infirmary to be upgraded out of social circumscription (the hospital began as an infirmary on Windmill Street)—pleas to the beneficence of a pocketwatch landlord, Mr. Goodge who, as early governor, overcame 'Vice' and 'Folly' to shell over the damp marshland.

For Sale: the Handel Ward fundraised by paraphernalia from a *Messiah* fundraiser at Westminster Abbey. Or other celebrity-staged oratorios—the Much Ado faultlessness of Garrick who could make a sumptuous bread from the ingredients in Shakespeare's granary. Or Dr. Arne of 'Rule Britannia' lordy-lore (a patriotic fanfare himself alone). Or the full-flasked pass-the-pot-enthusiasms of Samuel Whitbread, most liquefacient Anonymous benefactor, who knew the collusions between ale and hospital—101 dozen bottles of various plonks drunk by patients in 1820 (the warder's compassion for respite larks, or a kind of pre-anaesthetic indigene?)

The only visible remnant of the hospital is the far western wall—stripped and flimsy as a film set exterior. Fifty yards further East a small chapel deemed 'heritage' stands domitably unbridled, ripped loose from its congregation.

For Sale: the pre-hurricane zeal of Florence Nightingale's Middlesex apprenticeship. For the residents of Soho and Broad Street she practiced endless applications of terpentine stupes (she believed Cholera was not virulent from person to person). Only one nurse died during the outbreak.

Nightingale—immortalizing herself in Scutari—would forgo Matron Godiva who 'wielded absolute power absolutely'. A densely vigilant woman, at least one pair of her several stung black eyes constantly eyed up the nurses. (Godiva was also a remarkable cat hunter, killing any that she saw on sight, or running over the cabbage and kale yards to bag them up for the injection—'those little flea harbingers will bring this hospital to the ground', she said).

THE FOOTAGE

• Families will weep with joy tonight because your shower curtains are an ancient sign of prosperity.

• Housewives will peer into the vegetable glass of their refrigerators and feel a sense of suburban euphoria.

• Your livecams with Miss Latvia were prototyped into a fire alarm disguised as a rubber clock.

• Your knack for scooping wet soap beneath the shower's thunder is set to become a catalogue favourite.

• The pinched tears of your wife donning her black factory hat will weave a range of memorial curtains.

• Summer honeymooners will be offered a line of lingerie from the sleeping morass of your silk eiderdowns.

• The bridalware economy sings for you amid its certainty.

FOODSTUFFS

1.

In The Great Hall, with anvilled cutlery,
I feast at a table of illiberal foodies—
among them, the resplendently robust
colonel and his lemonfaced wife.
And I squawk, as they do, nefariously
galeing and regaling over a silent apéritif—
the bleached kelly green of twin avocados
sleekly peeled from their lute cases,
a jamboree of exotic oils meddling
in palisades of parmesan that sheen
the outercarriage of a butternut linguini.
Shall we eviscerate and equal the gods?

2.

The chef nods willingly, his rouge mouth
agape, braising shanks for the colonel,
who—to prevent further salivation—
makes an origami fan of his napkin,
stuffing it into the wattle of his throat.
Ahhh, foodstuffs, nostalgias the chef
and stares down at the struck lamb
with the saintliness of a demigod
who stares through the tessellated light
in a long mirror. *Little Lamb, I'll tell thee…*
of all that braises inside primal habit—
of happiness over function, meaning style.

3.

A tuxed ensemble of impeccable waiters
clear the mud-puddle of gravy plates,
returning with a regatta of cherry-brandied
chocolate fondue. The colonel's wife
mustachios herself with heavy cream and,
in the donnybrook of multiple servings,
she and the colonel eclipse the fondue
until all that remains are three split teeth
of biscotti. I peer deep into the chocpot
wondering what became of its flooded city.
The chef's heirloom, a soupçon, the table
and every guest, portentously menued.

ALL MOUTH

> Stars shine, and a wandering light
> Is kindled for the mourner, man.
> RANDALL JARRELL

all mouth	downwater	the moon
throwing	she said	white coins

[revision]

all mouth	she said	but tuppence
a yo-yoing	a plaything	countermined

[revision]

countersunk	she said	her conations
all mouth	like moons	gilt for pearl

[revision]

all peewit	she said	radish romance
all mouth	scallywag	all cloudtrousers

[revision]

all mouth	no trousers	like a moon
rear-vaulted	she said	sea-sanctified

[revision]

all mouth	she said	mirror-mournful
slug-abeds	all men	ghost-gladed

[revision]

oilskin moon	she said	grubby-white
all mouth	like men	full of wallow

RIMBAUD VILLANELLES

14 Rue Nicolet

What is wrong with the ex-pats and the French?
Only two of us show up for The Rimbaud Walk
despite the ballyhoo: *A 5 Mile Drift on Absinthe*.

Sure, there's a grin in the wind, but what prudence
nowadays; no surprise the UMP still shun a plaque
for 14 Rue Nicolet. What is wrong with the French?

Rimbaud, at sixteen, arrived here from the Ardennes
for havoc in the house of Verlaine's new stepparents,
and for Verlaine himself, who was gone on absinthe.

At night, they stumbled home under the low-lit lamps
surveyed by Verlaine's jilted *chanson*, Mathilde Mauté,
who despised the bad manners of these mountain French.

It is a house too prim for bohemians or boy peasants
agreed the in-laws. Lice-ridden, Rimbaud slept on the lawn
naked in the sun, peeled to his ribs, popeyed on absinthe.

Mathilde saw her life slide away whilst pregnant.
Verlaine threw little Georges at the wall and walked.
This house is a shamed house, censored by the French.
Before Rimbaud, Verlaine was hooked on absinthe.

Scarborough

Ashbery's *Illuminations* go delicately on Scarborough.
Prefacing his 'Promontoire', the old magpie sagely
implies that Rimbaud probably just read of Yorkshire,

'like the rest of us', who have never been to the Fair,
or skiffed parsley green docks at the harbour ferry.
I went, once. The coast is the prize of Scarborough,

its 'Royal' ledged up on steep hills from the harbour
like the 'Grand': odd facades twinned by 'Promontory',
as are Carthage and Brooklyn, Japan and Yorkshire.

Travel brochure hallucinations from the dream-digester,
assumes Robb, adding that 'Grand' ads were tabloidally
seen by Rimbaud, as likely to visit Glasgow as 'Scarbro'.

Yes, J.A., *Illuminations*: the hand of a psychogeographer
at the library. Why, then, did you timeout at the Q&A?
I claimed vision and you looked on, as if to Yorkshire,

guided by a scent of rosemary on the sea's tarantella,
the idea of a boy stock-seated, docking the promontory.
To arrive First Class, penniless, awash in Scarborough,
close your eyes, dodge the fare all the way to Yorkshire.

8 Royal College Street

Lot of the infernal bridegroom, of the red herring,
sold by a blind veterinary, then torn and desecrated
by Ogun and his vandal workmen. Attic of Verlaine

vs Rimbaud, where landlady Smith heard screaming
from her 'Parisian gentlemen', knife-tips slashed,
towel-wrapped, until the final slap of a wet herring.

The site endures because of months of campaigning:
McDevitt and Dun on the BBC, in Paris and *Le Monde*
assembling the French Embassy and, pro-Verlaine,

daring the council revamp no. 8 as a publishing
house with a floor where 'love must be re-invented'
and an absinthe bar. On the doorstep, grilled herring,

citations of 'Vagabonds', the formula still missing,
an ear pricked for the resale, hearing it landlorded
to Corby, a Camden Tory, who derided Verlaine,

if not Rimbaud, and would 'conserve' by subletting
no. 8, amiable still to a resident poet, so he pretended.
Capitalistically, Corby stuffed our ideas in a red herring.
For £1600 per week, cut-price: Rimbaud and Verlaine.

INSIDE THE HOUSE OF LU SAN

Inside the house of Lu San on Minn Street
a cat's paw swipes at a fishbowl and breaks
the trellis web between two toothbrushes—
nothing in the world is as mean as death.

Which does not mean the mildew-matted
base of a white metal bed, its edges stilted,
stretched beneath a bust of Christ / Socrates.

Twinned fragility: how the sculpture looms
above books dimmed in mahogany light,
from where she peek-a-boos, stage right—
concertina of a daughter, her little lobes

of feet stirring the kitchen's citrusy air.
A transbotanical face, shyly in soft focus—
life to the mythomania of life's possessions.

YOUR TOAD

for Maung Pyiyt Min

your toad that had toddled away
camouflaged by monsoon rain
reappears now at the edgewater
imperious as the lake herself

PLAYLIST

    Monsieur Le Maire De Niafunké

    how far to tread back

        —the grapes are too amiable
        the wine is overwrought—

    before the shrilling brass
        of antiquity

to where your interventionist
        god
            made
                havoc

    hammer to anvil
        of us
    memory to milk

    desire
    endstopped
    with
        violence

how far back

    to plummet
    into pure water

        pre-Athenian

            before the sweats
                of Gilgamesh

to where the spirit of the age
      was rivuleted

and you too
      were a rivulet
             monsieur

Mariama

trance of the polyglot

a single syllable's
hem and haw

>   a secret
>   whispered
>   behind
>   the hand

>   yet somehow
>   coherent

sound of market laughter

>   gruffly
>   echoic

as if a forest might speak
          to us
in the language of cutlery

knives of leaves
          from the etiological tree

that which replants itself
          from a single bud

>   and keeps growing
>   outwards

Kala Djula

cycloidal   the past

       undershadows

an afternoon of sun

       *

father at the window

       his hand

         self-effaced

too long

       waving

at its own reflection

Yombe

funerals over cards

women mourn
      men suit up
           for flushes

high stakes
      all this marking out
           of time

to marry one another's blindness

to forget
      what cannot be
           forgotten

the dream inside the coffin
           still lives

      the lacerated street
full of deathsmells

      but not sleeping

CHEIKH ANTA

so many ritual feasts
    yet still we are hungry

        trade wind fossil print
            on the riverglade

all these lives of sea
    filling out in our ears

NOTES

'Economies of The Living' was influenced by *Introduction to The English Reader* (1830), particularly sections called 'Didactic Pieces'.

'Phrase & Fable': all the subtitles in this sequence come from the *Brewer's Dictionary of Phrase and Fable*, Centenary Edition, Butler and Tanner Ltd., London, 1978.

'Pauperland': *Pauperland* is a book published by Jeremy Seabrook (Hurst & Co., London, 2013). *Pleonexia* in the pagan and early Christian era meant the morbid desire for possession.

'Playlist' is an auto-ekphrastic response to songs written and performed by Ali Farka Tourê & Toumani Diabatê, ('Monsieur Le Maire De Niafunké' and 'Kala Djula'), Nuru Kane ('Mariama' and 'Cheikh Anta') and Mokoomba ('Yombe'). The author does not speak any of the languages in which these songs were written.

BIOGRAPHICAL NOTE

James Byrne is a poet, editor, translator and Lecturer in Creative Writing at Edge Hill University. *Blood / Sugar* was published by Arc Publications in 2009 and in the same year he co-edited a seminal anthology of poets under 35 entitled *Voice Recognition: 21 Poets for the 21st Century* (Bloodaxe Books). In 2012 he also co-edited *Bones Will Crow: 15 Contemporary Burmese Poets*, published by Arc, the first anthology of Burmese poetry ever to be published in the West. Byrne is Editor of *The Wolf*, an internationally-renowned poetry magazine. He won the Treci Trg Poetry Festival prize in Serbia and his *Selected Poems: The Vanishing House* was published in Belgrade in 2009.

Now living in Liverpool, he graduated from New York University with an MFA, and is an NYU Stein Fellow ('Extraordinary International Scholar'). In 2011 he was the Poet in Residence at Clare Hall, University of Cambridge.

Byrne's poems have been translated into several languages, including Arabic, Burmese and Chinese and he is the International Editor for Arc Publications.

Selected titles in Arc Publications'
POETRY FROM THE UK / IRELAND include:

LIZ ALMOND
The Shut Drawer
Yelp!

D. M. BLACK
Claiming Kindred

JAMES BYRNE
Blood / Sugar

JONATHAN ASSER
Outside The All Stars

DONALD ATKINSON
In Waterlight:
Poems New, Selected & Revised

ELIZABETH BARRETT
A Dart of Green & Blue

JOANNA BOULTER
Twenty Four Preludes & Fugues on
Dmitri Shostakovich

THOMAS A CLARK
The Path to the Sea

TONY CURTIS
What Darkness Covers
The Well in the Rain
folk

JULIA DARLING
Sudden Collapses in Public Places
Apology for Absence

LINDA FRANCE
You are Her

KATHERINE GALLAGHER
Circus-Apprentice
Carnival Edge

RICHARD GWYN
Sad Giraffe Café

GLYN HUGHES
A Year in the Bull-Box

MICHAEL HASLAM
The Music Laid Her Songs in Language
A Sinner Saved by Grace
A Cure for Woodness

MICHAEL HULSE
The Secret History
Half-Life

CHRISTOPHER JAMES
Farewell to the Earth

BRIAN JOHNSTONE
The Book of Belongings
Dry Stone Work

JOEL LANE
Trouble in the Heartland
The Autumn Myth

HERBERT LOMAS
The Vale of Todmorden
A Casual Knack of Living
COLLECTED POEMS

SOPHIE MAYER
(O)

PETE MORGAN
August Light

MICHAEL O'NEILL
Wheel
Gangs of Shadow

MARY O'DONNELL
The Ark Builders

IAN POPLE
An Occasional Lean-to
Saving Spaces

PAUL STUBBS
The Icon Maker
The End of the Trial of Man

LORNA THORPE
A Ghost in My House
Sweet Torture of Breathing

ROISIN TIERNEY
The Spanish-Italian Border

MICHELENE WANDOR
Musica Transalpina
Music of the Prophets
Natural Chemistry

JACKIE WILLS
Fever Tree
Commandments
Woman's Head as Jug